Are you sociable like a dolphin or shy like a seahorse?

CURIOUS Questions & answers about... Our Oceans

What's your favourite colour?

Do you prefer swimming or skating?

If you could eat one food every day what would it be?

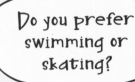

If you could chat to a whale or a walrus, which would you choose?

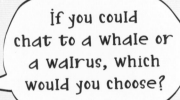

What's your FAVOURITE ocean animal?

Words by Camilla de la Bédoyère

Illustrations by Tim Budgen

MILES KELLY

How big is an ocean?

There are five oceans and they are all HUGE! Together, they cover two thirds of Earth's surface.

NORTH AMERICA

ATLANTIC OCEAN

An ocean is a large area of salty water. It's also called the sea.

PACIFIC OCEAN

SOUTH AMERICA

Seaweeds are plants that live in salty water.

Day octopus

SOUTHERN OCEAN

Long-snouted seahorse

Are the oceans important?

Yes, billions of animals and plants live in them! People use the things that live in the ocean for all sorts of things, too. A type of seaweed called red algae is used in peanut butter – it makes it easy to spread!

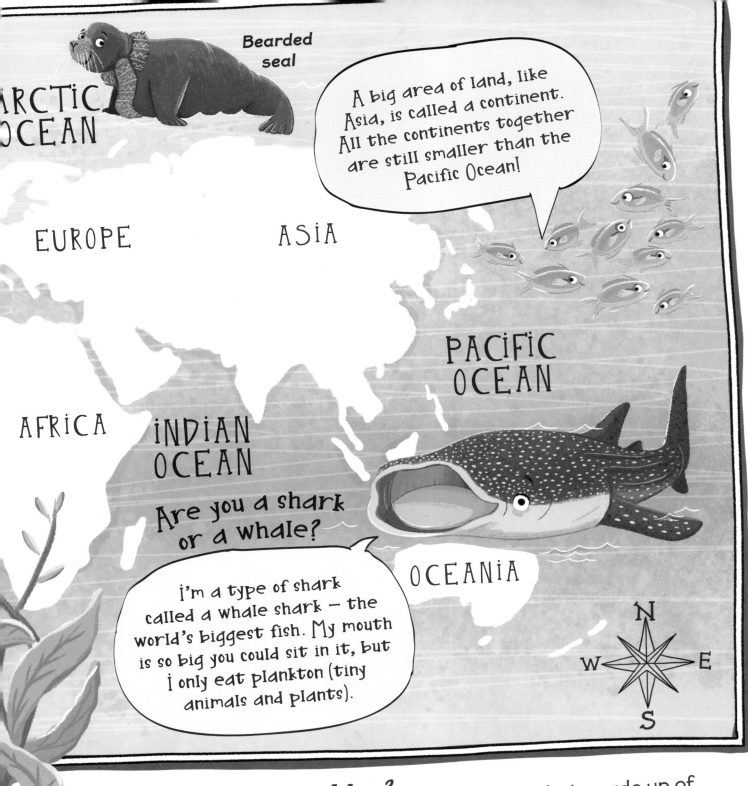

Bearded seal

ARCTIC OCEAN

A big area of land, like Asia, is called a continent. All the continents together are still smaller than the Pacific Ocean!

EUROPE

ASIA

PACIFIC OCEAN

AFRICA

INDIAN OCEAN

Are you a shark or a whale?

OCEANIA

I'm a type of shark called a whale shark – the world's biggest fish. My mouth is so big you could sit in it, but I only eat plankton (tiny animals and plants).

N
W E
S

Why is the sea blue?

Sunlight is made up of lots of colours. When it shines on the ocean, most of the colours disappear into the water, but blue light bounces back, so the ocean looks blue.

What is a fish?

Fish are animals that have skeletons, gills and fins. There are more than 32,000 types, and most of them live in oceans.

Tail fin swishes from side to side when swimming

Overlapping scales are smooth and slippery

Herring

Slim, sleek body moves quickly through water

I'm the perfect shape for swimming. My silvery scales help water to flow easily over my skin.

Can people breathe underwater too?

No – sorry! You need to breathe air because you have lungs. All fish have special organs called gills that work in water.

Water and air have oxygen gas in them. All animals need oxygen to live.

Oxygen-rich water flows in

Water flows out over the gills, where the oxygen passes into the fish's blood

Triggerfish

Do fish have special homes?

Some do. Clownfish live among the tentacles of stinging sea anemones. The fish are covered in special slime that protects them from stings, but animals that might want to eat them can't get close!

Can fish fly?

No – but some can glide. Flying fish have very streamlined bodies and use their big fins to launch out of the water into the air.

I can glide for up to 200 metres.

Whoosh!

How is my nose like a shark?

Most fish skeletons are made of bone. Shark skeletons are made of cartilage, which is softer than bone. Our noses and ears have cartilage – that's why they're bendy!

Bull shark

Did you know?

A **hairy frogfish** is a fast eater. It sucks food into its mouth like a vacuum cleaner – 50 times faster than the blink of an eye!

At 3 metres long, the ocean **sunfish** is one of the world's biggest bony fish.

Octopuses can turn red when they are angry.

Electric rays can zap fish with an electric shock. Once the fish has been stunned, the ray can eat it!

Seaweed is often used as a thickener in ice cream!

The **sperm whale** has the biggest brain on the planet – and probably the whole Universe!

500 million years ago the only living things on Earth were in the ocean.

Baby sharks and baby seals are called **pups**, and baby fish are called **fry**.

Shark skin feels like sandpaper. It is covered in tiny bumpy scales that help them slip through the water.

I'm more like a hippo than a herring!

Whales and **dolphins** aren't fish – they are mammals.

A **great white shark** can eat enough meat to make 3000 burgers in one go, and it won't want to eat again for at least ten days.

North Pole

Polar bears and **penguins** never meet because penguins live near the South Pole and polar bears live near the North Pole!

It's like looking in a mirror!

South Pole

Sailors used to think that **dugongs** were mermaids. They're actually plump mammals that spend their time grazing on sea plants.

Do trees grow in the deep sea?

No – but giant kelp seaweed grows in huge forests! It is found in the Pacific Ocean, and can grow up to 50 centimetres in one day.

Bumps contain air that helps the kelp to float

A kelp forest is a great place to hide – one strand can be more than 30 metres long.

We are lizards that live on the Galapagos Islands in the Pacific Ocean.

Who picnics at the bottom of the sea?

Marine iguanas do! They dive to depths of 12 metres – and stay there for up to an hour while they nibble on seaweed that grows on the seabed.

Do baby fish go to nursery?

Young fish and reptiles keep away from predators in special hiding places called nurseries. Shallow waters around sea grasses and mangrove tree roots make good nurseries.

Sea otters can wrap themselves in kelp so they don't float away

Mangrove trees grow at the coast, with their roots in shallow salty water.

Sea creatures sometimes mistake plastic floating in the ocean for food. If we eat it, it can kill us.

What do turtles eat?

Green sea turtles feast on fields of sea grasses that grow underwater.

Baby turtles hide from sharks in the sea grasses

Who plays hide and seek?

Many ocean animals do! On coral reefs, millions of sea creatures live close together. Lots of them use clever tricks to avoid being eaten by the others.

I look like seaweed. I'm a type of fish called a leafy seadragon.

I'm a sea slug – aren't I beautiful? My lovely colours tell animals that I am poisonous.

I'm a decorator crab, and I'm holding onto a piece of coral as a clever disguise.

I'm a cuttlefish and I can change colour in a flash.

Do fish need friends?

My best friend is a busy little shrimp. I'm a coral grouper and my friend cleans my teeth.

I also nibble away any dead skin. Yum!

We moray eels have long, thin bodies and can hide in cracks in the coral. We eat almost anything we can catch.

Can you see a reef from space?

Yes! The Great Barrier Reef stretches over 2000 kilometres off the coast of Australia. Reefs are built by tiny animals called polyps. Each one lives in its own rocky cup, waving its tentacles in the water.

It took thousands of years for polyps like me to build the Great Barrier Reef.

How long does it take to make an island?

If a volcano erupts on the seabed, it can make an island in a few years! Lava (a type of liquid rock) pours out and builds up to create a brand new island.

Volcano erupts on seabed

A cone shape of lava forms on the seabed

The cone grows so big it breaks the surface – it's a new island!

Can I find treasure on an island?

Yes – but not the sort that belongs to pirates! The treasure to be found on islands is all the precious animals that live on them.

We're baby hawksbill turtles. Our mum laid eggs in a nest and then swam away. Now we're hatching.

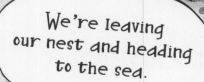

We're leaving our nest and heading to the sea.

I fly to islands when it's time to build my nest and lay eggs. I'm an albatross, and I'm huge.

Black and white ruffed lemur

Who lives on an island?

Islands are often home to animals that live nowhere else on Earth. About 60 types of lemur live only on the island of Madagascar, which is in the Indian Ocean.

Christmas Island, near Australia, swarms with millions of red crabs. We lay our eggs in the sea.

Giant tortoises like me are found on coral islands in the Indian Ocean. We can live to be more than 100 years old!

How many?

About **100 million** sharks are killed by people every year.

I'm one of the longest animals ever!

10 metres The length of a bootlace worm.

400 million

The number of years that sharks have lived in the oceans.

There are more volcanoes under the sea than on land! **452** are on the edges of the Pacific Ocean.

Pufferfish have poisonous flesh. About **30** people die every year after eating them.

7 metres

The length of the biggest saltwater crocodiles.

A single one of my teeth can be more than 10 centimetres in length!

A starfish can have more than **30** arms!

There were **40 million** crabs on Christmas Island – until yellow crazy ants arrived. They spray the crabs with acid and eat them, so far killing about **15 million** of them.

My arms are covered with hundreds of tiny feet. I use them to walk on the seabed.

507

...the incredible age in years of a clam that was found in the Atlantic Ocean.

Phew!

40,000

...the number of eggs a herring can lay in one go.

A narwhal's giant tooth can reach **3 metres** in length.

350
The number of types of coral that live in the Great Barrier Reef.

That's why it's important to cut down the amount of plastic you use, and to recycle it.

1 million
seabirds are killed every year by plastic rubbish that is in the ocean.

Who sleeps in a muddy bed?

Sea cucumbers do! These slug-like animals live in mud, eat mud and poo mud! Sea cucumbers are animals, not vegetables, but some people do like to eat them!

I'm a longnose sawshark. I hunt fish and crabs that are hiding in the mud. My nose is lined with sharp teeth!

The bottom of the sea is covered in mud and sand. It's called the seabed!

How do people explore under the sea?

People can't breathe in water, but we still find ways to explore the deep ocean. We can scuba dive, use submarines, or send robots with cameras.

I'm a glowing jellyfish called a mauve stinger.

Remotely operated underwater vehicles are one way for people to explore deep water from the safety of the surface

Who lights up the deep, dark sea?

Sunlight can't reach the bottom of the deep sea. So some animals make their own light instead!

Who stands on three legs?

Tripod fish have three long, leg-like fins to stand on the seabed. Each fin-leg can be more than 50 centimetres long! Then they keep their mouths open and wait for food to swim right in.

Viperfish like me use flashing lights to attract little animals to swim close. Then we swallow them up! My mouth is so big I can swallow animals bigger than me!

Puffin

Why does the sea go in and out?

Over the course of a day at the seaside you will see the sea moving in and out. This is called the tide, and it's caused by the Moon!

When the tide is in, the shore is covered with water. When the tide is out, there's still some water left in rock pools. How many animals can you see living here?

Eel

Brittlestar

Goby

Why is there jelly in a rock pool?

Hermit crab

I'm not jelly, I'm a beadlet anemone! When the tide is in, my tentacles wave in the water. When it goes out I fold my tentacles in so I look like a wobbly blob!

Who loves to surf?

Humans – but dolphins ride the waves too! Flat water turns to waves when wind blows over the top of it.

Which animals go to school?

We do! Young orcas like us have to learn to catch our lunch! Our mums take us to shallow water to show us how to hunt shoals of fish, seals and baby whales.

lumpsucker

Who snacks at the shore?

Grey seals feed on all kinds of animals near the shore, from crabs to seabirds. They can also dive to depths of 70 metres when hunting.

Would you rather?

Which would you prefer – soaring with a **sea eagle** or surfing with a **penguin**?

I soar on 2-metre-wide wings, plucking sea snakes and turtles out of the water.

I use my wings like flippers to swim and leap through the waves.

My big mouth is full of eggs! After my mate lays them I keep them safe in my mouth until they hatch.

Would you rather be covered in spikes like a **pineapplefish** or have a huge mouth like a **jawfish**?

Would you rather be a **marine biologist** and study ocean animals, or a **marine geologist** and find out all about the mysterious seabed?

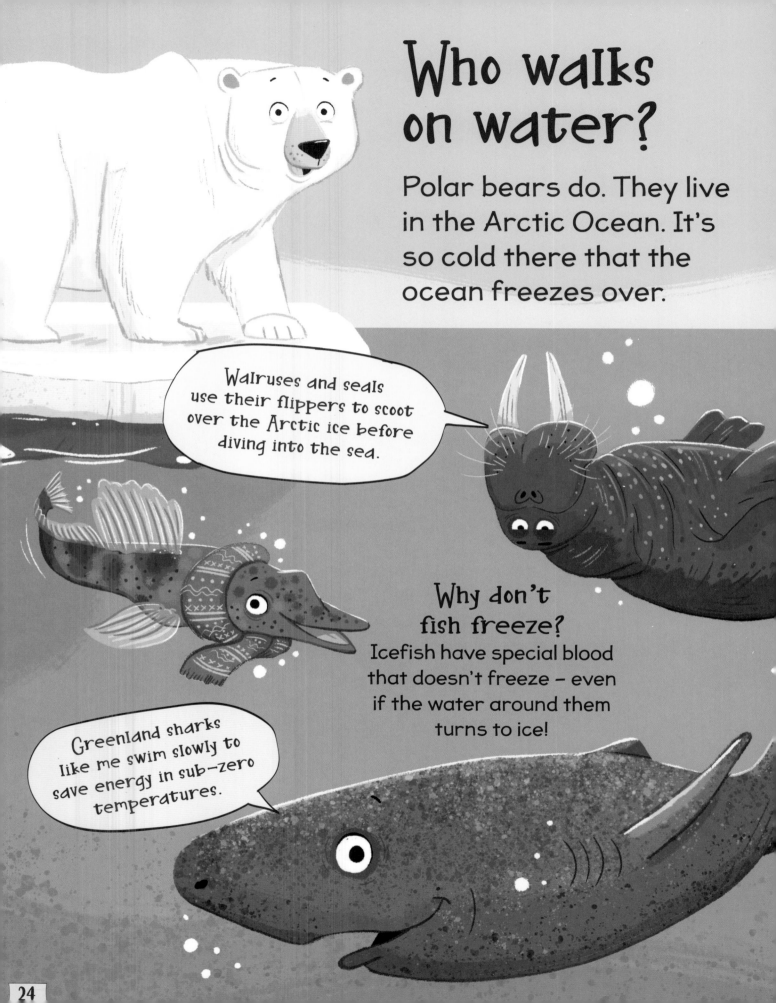

Who walks on water?

Polar bears do. They live in the Arctic Ocean. It's so cold there that the ocean freezes over.

Walruses and seals use their flippers to scoot over the Arctic ice before diving into the sea.

Why don't fish freeze?
Icefish have special blood that doesn't freeze – even if the water around them turns to ice!

Greenland sharks like me swim slowly to save energy in sub-zero temperatures.

Why do icebergs float?

Icebergs are made of frozen water. Ice is lighter than water, so it floats. Big sheets of ice float on the sea too. They are good places for penguins and seals to take a nap when they are tired of swimming, slipping and sliding!

Where did that seal go?

Under the ice — I'm brilliant at holding my breath! We Weddell seals only have to poke our heads up through holes in the ice once an hour to get air.

Who sings beautiful songs in the cold sea?

I do! I'm a white beluga whale and I sing so loudly that people in boats can hear my lovely songs.

Who packs a powerful punch?

I'm only the size of your foot, but I can smash a thick sheet of glass.

A peacock mantis shrimp is one of the world's strongest animals for its size! It uses its club-like legs to wallop other animals at lightning speed.

Sting!

Which fish has the most vicious venom?

I do! I'm an Indian stonefish. I have 13 sharp spines on my back to inject the venom, and it's strong enough to kill a human. I use this clever trick to protect myself from attack.

Why do jellyfish sting?

A jellyfish uses its long, stinging tentacles to get a meal. Each tentacle carries tiny, venomous darts that jab passing fish prey.

I'm a box jellyfish – the most dangerous jellyfish in the world. I have enough venom to kill 60 people!

Who can smell a drop of blood in the sea?

Sharks can! These incredible hunters have a super sense of smell that helps them find fish and other animals to eat.

Sniff!

Hammerhead sharks have strange heads. This odd shape helps us to see and smell animals, and to swim fast.

One tentacle can grow more than 20 metres long!

Are there monsters in the sea?

There are some very big animals in the sea... but no monsters. From huge rays and outsize crabs to the biggest animal on Earth – plenty of giants lurk in the deep.

Why do whales spout water?

That's how they breathe! Whales breathe air. They all have one or two blowholes, which are like nostrils. A spout from a whale is really just a big, warm, wet breath!

Which crab has the longest legs?

A Japanese spider crab has 10 legs, and each leg can be over 2 metres long! These mega crabs can reach 100 years old.

What's the biggest animal?

Me! I'm also the biggest animal to ever live! I can grow up 25 metres long and my tongue weighs the same as an elephant.

A compendium of questions

Can I drink seawater?

No – it can make you sick. Seawater is too salty, and often dirty too. The dirt is called pollution and it's bad for all living things.

Can I swim across an ocean?

No human has ever swum across one without taking a break in a boat. But whales, sharks and turtles can!

Why do thresher sharks have such long tails?

They use the enormous upper lobes of their tail fins to wallop shoals of their fish prey.

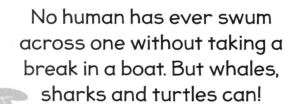

Which fish ties itself in knots?

A hagfish! It's covered in slippery slime and ties itself in knots when it is feasting on dead animals at the bottom of the sea.

How smart is an octopus?

An octopus can work out how to open a jar to reach food inside! It uses its suckers to grip shellfish and rip them open.